MW00605745

if only God and i saw it....the show was worth staging®

if only God and i saw it... the show was worth staging®

haiku
and
images
by
tony corcetto

act 1

first edition: november 2003

library of congress control number 2003091345
isbn 0-9722901-3-3
slipcased limited edition: isbn 0-9722901-8-4

cover and interior design by tony corcetto
digital scans of photos by dcc photo, wyomissing, pa 19610
typeface throughout is adobe poetica—designed by robert slimbach

published by skywind publishing, 3 skywind drive, reinholds, pa 17569

printed in singapore

humbly

dedicated

to my

companion,

God,

the

master

show

producer.

the show goes on theater-in-the-round . . . in reverse. • we are positioned center stage with the set ever changing around us . . . rain and snow . . . winter and summer . . . morning and night . . . close-ups and vistas . . . on and on. • and to enjoy this spectacular show, we need to do merely that . . . enjoy it! • open our eyes. • open our minds. • let our thoughts meander. • boredom will never be in the lexicon of one who does so. • my wish for this book is that the reader finds it spiritually uplifting and it engenders awareness and humility when taking in the wonders of the great stage with which we have been blessed.

haiku defined. haiku is a short form of verse which has been popular with japanese poets for centuries. • it originated as the first three lines of a five-line poem called a tanka which was written by two people as a game. • one person wrote the first three lines called a hokku, and the other replied with the final two. • the hokku eventually became popular as a form on its own and as such it is properly called a haiku. • in this volume, i have married pho-tography to the haiku. • whereas haiku often includes a clue to the season within it, i've chosen for the photos to carry that message • the haiku is made up of three lines of seventeen syllables. • the first and third lines have five syllables each, and the second line seven. • this rigidity of form contrasts with the opportunity for the imagination to ramble freely while interpreting the words and imagery. • you're invited to write your own haiku to accompany the photos. • imagine. • explore . . .

acknowledgements as i progressed on this book, i showed page proofs to a number of people. their sincere reactions were heartwarming and convinced me i had created something special and worth pursuing. to try to list them all would risk the chance of missing someone. in lieu of that, i will thank them in person. nonetheless, they know who they are and should know i am truly grateful for their contribution to inspiring me in my work.

an artistic goose.

abstract expressionism

rippling in its wake.

a bouquet of hues.

safeguarded behind a fence

of barbs and brambles.

through a veil of flakes,

we peep as the doe snuggles

on fresh sheets of white.

Shakespeare would love it.

what a great backdrop for the

dane's soliloquy!

and when the rain comes,

to whom will the may apple

lend its umbrella?

a pine cone confined

in a frigid ice cocoon.

hurry, sun, free it.

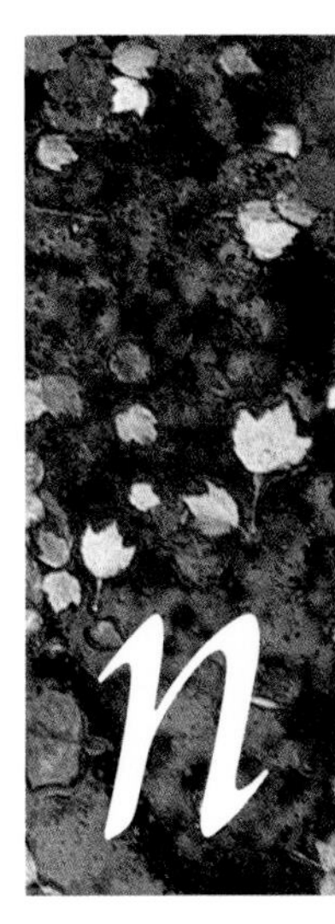

N aked, the maple

sees her reflection mingling

with her castoff leaves.

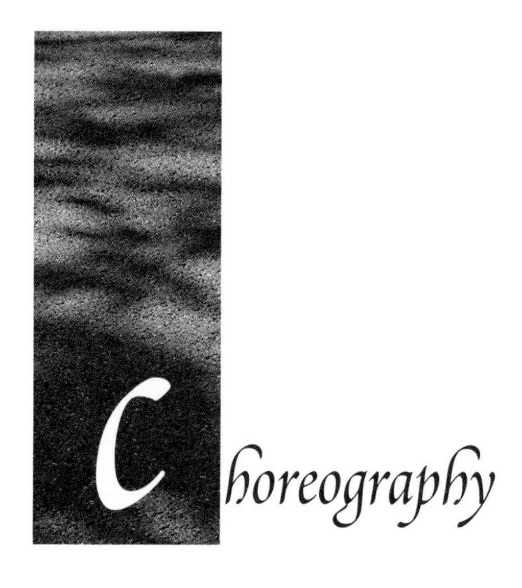

Choreography

courtesy of the west wind.

leaf shadows dancing.

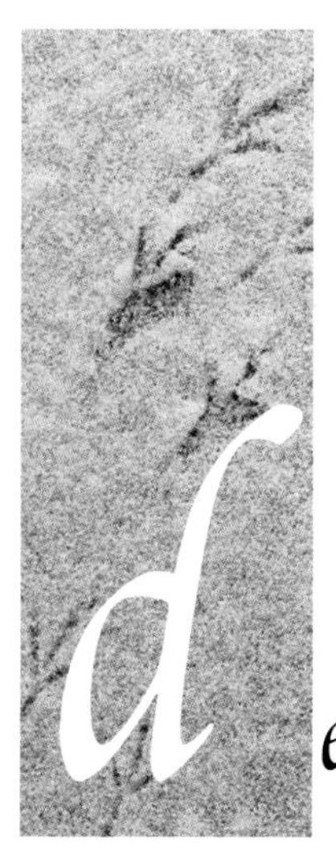

devilish titmouse,

must you scribble grafitti

in the newborn snow?

Imperceptibly,

the ivy army invades

the brick battlefield.

nsconced on his throne

of tube and canvas. content.

ruler of his realm.

Window gallery.

each pane its own work of art...

shifting with the light.

102

down from the heavens,

nestled on weathered creek stones,

wisps of frozen clouds.

The torrents of spring.

rivers of gold splash across

undulating fields.

Scattered above us,

hidden as we bide our days...

galaxy of nails.

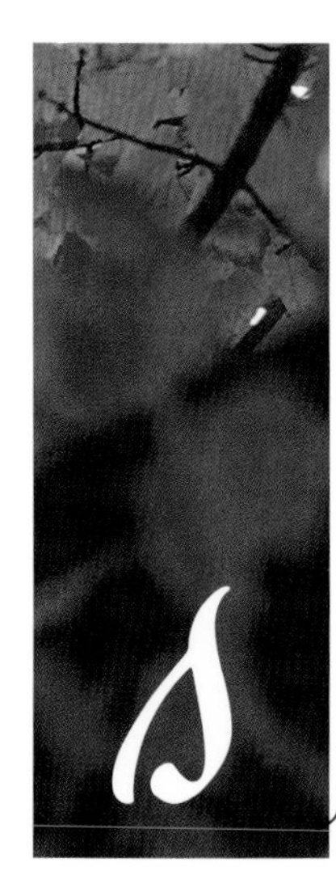

Spellbinding colors.

the fall leaves astonish us,

and then...old glory!

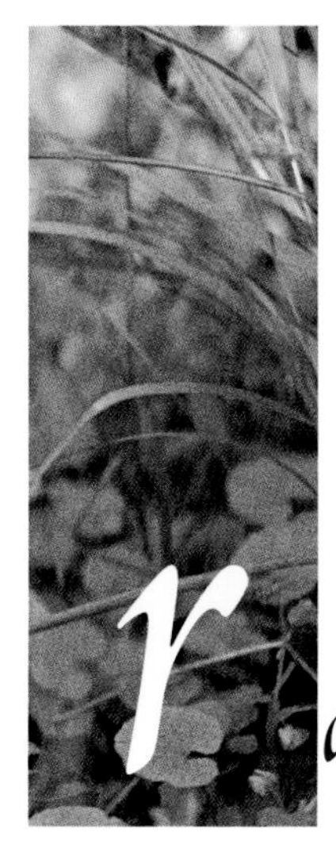

r abbit in heaven.

to the north, east, south and west...

scrumptious green salad.

how appropriate!

midst the branches capped with snow,

what else? a snowbird.

olden chariots,

ready to shepherd our most

precious possessions.

SCHOOL BUS
SCHOOL BUS
SCHOOL BUS
SCHOOL BUS
311

Caution! lurking there

mid the virginia creeper—

vile poison ivy.

What a romantic!

everywhere it goes, the deer

prints us valentines.

"Okay, get with it!

this pose shows my best profile.

please snap the shutter!"

the sycamore clings

to its cache of ornaments

and waits for christmas.

Comforting beauty

softens the blow to come of

bills, bills, and more bills.

15 Laurel Lane

ound frozen...as is.

she mourned not, but proffered us

her last pirouette.

refresh your freedom.

every once in a blue moon,

park outside the lines.

Poised perilously

'twixt worlds of earth and water,

we walk life's tightrope.

Small, lonely blossom,

fear not that you've bloomed in vain.

i see you down there!

Melting, pristine snow.

mother earth peeks out with her

craggy, textured face.

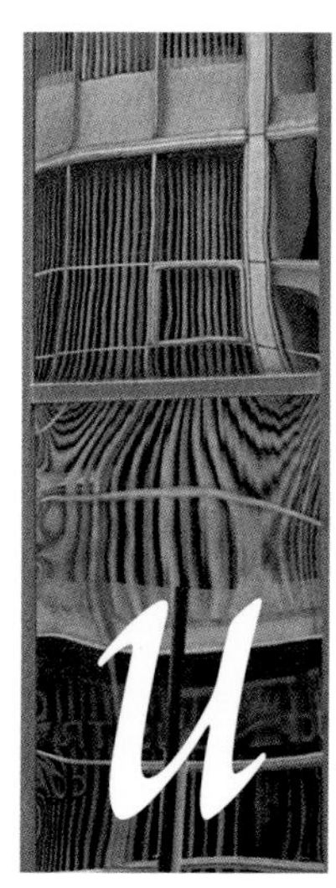

Urban reflections

of the human comedy.

huge funhouse mirrors.

NO
STOPPING
7-9AM
4-6PM
1 HOUR
PARKING
9AM-4PM
NO PARKING

n the hollow core

of a tree stump, a leaf finds

shelter from the wind.

Tiny butterfly

transforming scenes to beauty

wherever you rest.

Like a general,

the oak steels the woodland troops

to defy the storm.

antique handmade panes.

misty prisms, reflecting

the autumn grandeur.

a crowd of blossoms.

so fragile, yet strong enough

to chase the winter.

echo of autumn.

a solitary leaf rests

on rain dimpled snow.

eavens, what a slob!

munching, while standing on the

very food he eats.

Patiently waiting,

perched in the woodland tangle—

expectant father.

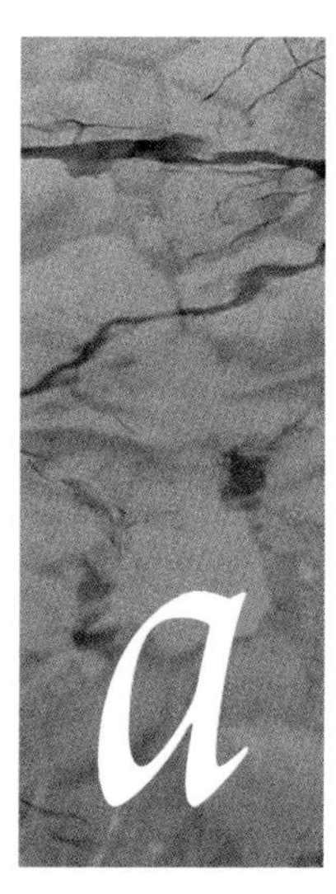

a rich tapestry—

woven from muted threads of

air, earth and water.

Proud, its head held high,

despite the wind forever

blowing in its face.

you there, in my sink.

the faucet niagara

is coming. scurry!

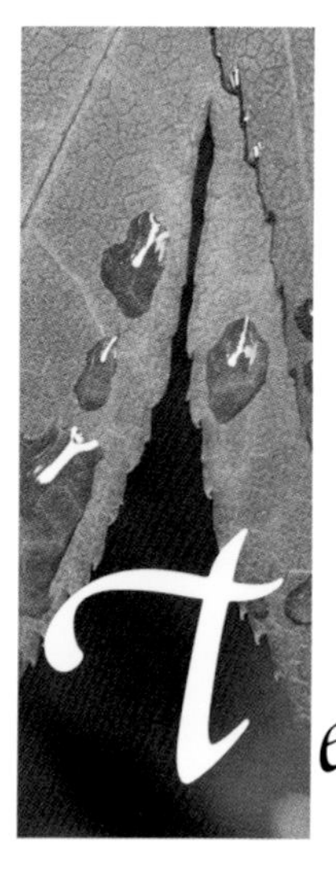ears mix with raindrops

as the thirsty plants rejoice!

the drought has ended.

lown hither and yon,

always bending with the flow,

it lands uninjured.

ebbing and flowing,

the wind wafts through the holly

humming... "si-lent night..."

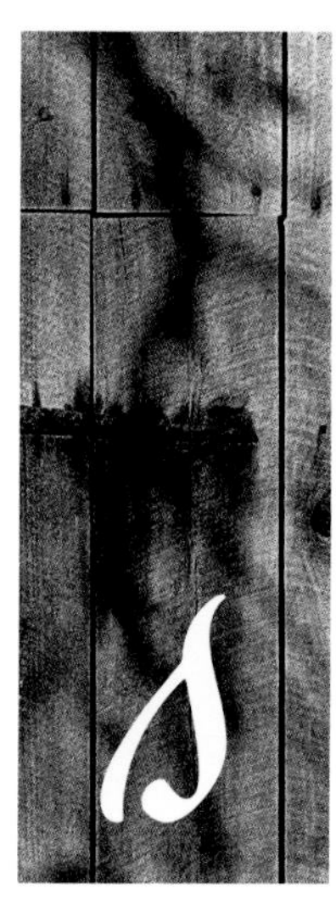hadows and siding.

cousins. both arboreal

in their ancestry.

from its stump, the tree

offers up its last hurrah—

a funeral spray.

Upon a canvas,

reminiscent of monét,

some more daubs of white.

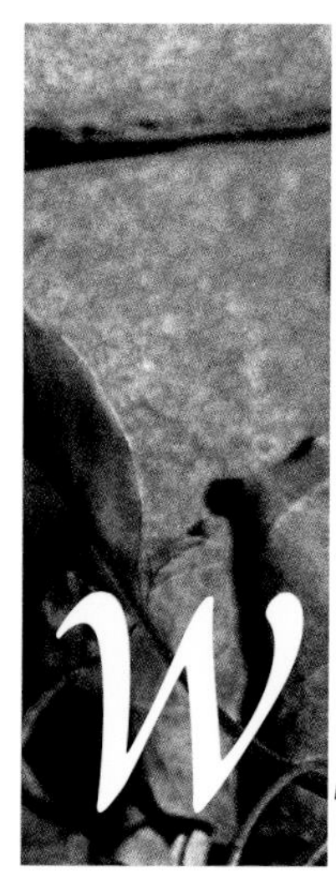

What warrior ghost

lies lurking within this stone?

see his warpaint stripes.

After a season

weathered by the elements,

tarnished green gone gold.

Are you envious?

if only your children were

as well disciplined.

Ontelaunee foam,

beyond the spillway plunge, rests

by the rocky shore.

ontelaunee is a lake in berks county, pennsylvania.

fter the shower,

the white pine is bejeweled.

glittering sequins.

“gang! we’ve got a gig.

there’s this director, hitchcock,

making a movie...”

Such an exotic

playground in which to frolic.

oh! to be...a bee.

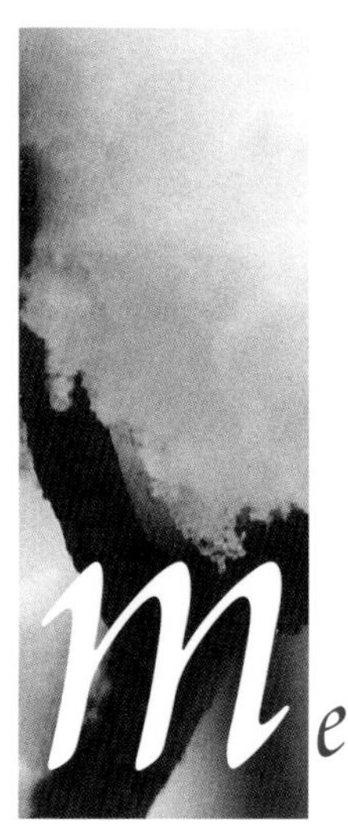

Metamorphosis.

snow twists and turns on a twig.

white caterpillar.

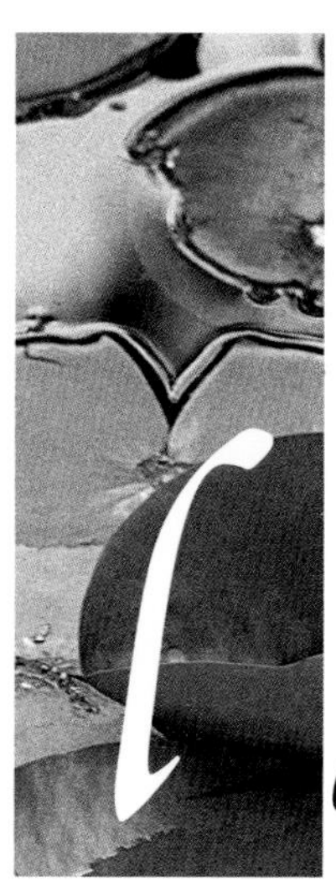ady lily pad,

gossip of the neighborhood

in your new fall hat.

a hole in the wall.

we add stones: one large, one small.

then behold! a crèche!

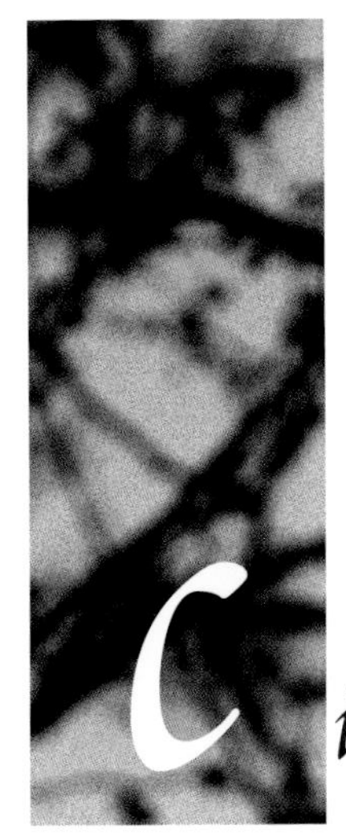

Circling. admiring.

an infatuated swain.

earth's constant lover.

Vast ocean of leaves.

quickly! shuck your shoes and socks

and skip in its surf.

After the dark...dawn.

a baby day bursts forth with

possibilities.

pax

vobiscum